CW00545660

OLDBURY:
The Town of the
Four Moons

the story of Oldbury in extract and anecdote
compiled and edited by Dave Reeves

© 1994

**Published by The Moving Finger for
Sandwell Community Library Service**
Oldbury Library
Church Street
Oldbury
Warley
West Midlands
B69 3AF
ISBN 1 871296 55 2
Design and Layout - The Moving Finger, PO Box 2923,
WARLEY, West Midlands, B67 5AG.
Front Cover Design and Layout - Sakab Bashir
Printing - Genesis Europrint, Olton Wharf, Solihull, B92 7RN.

Photographs courtesy of:

      Pg 5   Sandwell Community Libraries (Photographer: F.Wakeman)
      Pg 11 As Above (Postcard published by Roden & Son)
      Pg 16 Alf Parkes
      Pg 19 Sandwell Community Libraries (Photographer: H.L.Jenkins)
      Pg 25 Accles and Pollock
      Pg 30 Mrs Conley
      Pg 32 S.Screen
      Pg 36 M.Price

Front Cover Photographs: Tank - Accles & Pollock; Polly on the Fountain - as
Pg. 19; London Works, Halesowen St, from Parish Church Tower 1948 - Sandwell
Community Libraries (Photographer: M.Wyatt).

Copyright © 1994
Individual copyright © remains with the authors, photographers and designers.
All attempts have been made to trace copyright holders. Where we have been
unsuccessful we would be glad to hear from them and to include this information
in future editions.

British Library Cataloguing-in-Publication Data.
A catalogue record for this book is available from the British Library.

This book is published with
the financial assistance of
Sandwell Arts Development

INTRODUCTION

This book was never meant as a precise history of Oldbury, more as a celebration of the town. It was first dreamt of by Thelma Prentice, then Community Librarian at Oldbury Library, during a creative writing residency which I undertook there.

During that residency a number of pieces of both creative writing and reminiscence were written some during workshops organised in the library, some with school-children from two local schools. I was asked to edit a selection of that writing together with reminiscences that we had gathered and extracts from other already published works about Oldbury. Here is the result. There was much more that I could have talked about, more detail I could have gone into, but I feel that those who become intrigued, as I have become, can use this as a starting point for their own researches.

Dave Reeves

Thanks

Thanks are due to:- Jubilee Community Arts for use of equipment; Paul Rollason of Accles & Pollock; Thelma Prentice for instigating the book; David Gill, Kate Millin and Alison Gill for steering the project; Jessica Harris, Sandwell Arts Development for funding; John Maddison, Sandwell Local Studies Officer for his invaluable assistance in tracing information; Kath West for help in gathering information; and to all those who contributed writing, reminiscences and photographs.

About the Editor

Dave Reeves is a freelance writer, performer and editor who was born in the Black Country. He has undertaken numerous community writing projects and is known for his work with Writing and Primary Healthcare. The Times Saturday Review described him as "a kind of cultural hired gun". He is a founder member of 'The Moving Finger'.

CONTENTS

Church Street Bridge.

OLDBURY ON CUT

Khanyer Whackett

In April 1949, Mr George Isaacs (then Minister for Labour) came to Oldbury to open 'Made In Oldbury' an exhibition of local industrial effort (see Pg. 23). This poem was written to welcome him.

When I first came to Oldbury,
It was not upon the map;
And when I asked the reason why
Was told 'twas on the back.
We see that smaller towns galore
Are on the maps we get,
But "Oldbury" - though I often look,
Have failed to find it yet.

In fifty years the progress made
Has really been so good,
My plea "a place upon the map"
Is easily understood.
But though the fact that on the maps
Our town they just ignore,
The work that's done in Oldbury counts
It is known the whole world o'er.

But here you are in Oldbury,
You found the way all right,
If you trusted to an England map
We wondered if you might.
But now you're here we welcome you
And trust you will enjoy
This - our Century celebration
As the evening passes by.

We hear of towns as "on the Thames"
Some the Severn and Avon choose
And there is one that's on the Trent
Quite noted for its booze.
There is Birmingham, that's on the Rea
Not a noble river - but
They are really better off than us
For we only have the "Cut".

'Khanyer Whackett' was the pen name of W.W.Hackett the first foreman of Accles & Pollock who rose to became Managing Director. He was well known for his "leg-pulling" in verse and sold books of his work to raise funds for the local 'Sons of Rest'. (see Pg. 25).

THE BEST SLEDGING IN THE UNIVERSE   *Brian Counley*

Oldbury is where I live. It is not a town, really; more of a village. A trip to the shops which should take ten minutes takes almost an hour as one 'bumps' into friends who ask you, "Did you know that old Charlie ....." The 'developer' has already built a huge hypermarket which, when it was completed in 1980, echoed the boast of its management that it was the largest in the country. I, for one, believed them. After all, in the process of being built it gobbled up a number of streets which had housed a busy bus terminus; a Victorian edifice the locals called 'la pom' and Sanders furniture store where I was sent, as a young lad, to fetch the heavy lead accumulator battery which powered our crackling radio set; a school; two chapels; the old public library; half the old Town Hall and a barbers shop.

British Rail, not to be outdone, tore down the little railway station with its wooden floor that echoed hollowly under one's tread to the booking office window. They demolished the cosy wooden waiting room with its coal fire and erected an endless concrete platform costing over £2 million and called it 'Sandwell & Dudley'. No mention of Oldbury, and Dudley happens to be about four miles away - much to the consternation of those passengers who alight here and expect to find Dudley at the bottom of the station steps.

But the farce does not end there. The grand opening of Sandwell and Dudley Station demanded that all the top brass should assemble to welcome in the very first train. Perhaps the driver had been told to stop at Oldbury and, like most other rail users, got a little confused by the new title, for he sped past the open mouthed dignitaries awaiting him on the platform and disappeared in a cloud of dust, over the horizon towards Birmingham New Street.

Oldbury: its very name suggests antiquity, being a derivation of 'Old burh', so they say. If that is the case, it would mean that Anglo-Saxons found it an ancient, and perhaps deserted, British settlement. It would have been in existence many hundreds of years before they came across it. The Anglo-Saxons named it Ealdanbyrig and, in Middle English tongue the name was changed to Aldebury. There is a road not far from my home called Penncricket Lane which is an ancient county boundary. Penncricket was a name given to the end of a boundary by the British over two thousand years ago. From my window I can see Bury Hill, green and mysterious and wonder at all that gentle rising greenness, a place of summer picnics, which was once a violent slab of seething molten volcanic lava. When I walk on Bury Hill, two lines of Spencers 'A Hymn In Honour Of Beauty' always predominate my thoughts:

> "That beauty is not, as fond men misdeem
> An outward show of things, that only seem".

The beauty of Bury Hill is both intangible and exasperating. It certainly does not inspire the muse within with its wild magnificence - as do the gaunt and rocky crags of Wales or Scotland. There are no silvery waterfalls glinting over precipitous cliffs to charge the blood with adrenalin. And to climb the summit is not unduly laborious and only increases the breathing rate by a couple of notches. Yet, time and time again, I return to climb its grassy slopes. The hill fascinates me. Its origins are volcanic. Thrown up from the bowels of the earth it is the largest slab of lava left in the West Midlands.

Standing there on this placid September morning with the breeze just strong enough to ruffle one's hair; there is a certain exhilaration, a link with pre-history which gives one a sense of stability in a world very far from stable. And there is a certain, satisfactory irony about Bury Hill. Born of fire it is fitting that it protects a town born of the same element. Older than man, it has watched us, born from the same mother, grow, mature and prosper. Coal, steel and iron, trinity of Black Country wealth and all dependent on fire; fire so fierce and awesome that legend has it that the devil himself, standing, perhaps, on the very spot which I now stand, looked about in amazement and henceforth regarded the fires of hell as nothing more than ordinary.

The wind that bends the grass also whispers of another legend. Folklore has it that a castle once stood here, inhabited by the Lady Brade - said to be the daughter of Roger de Mortumare, Sheriff of Shropshire. Her sweetheart, Ralph, Lord of Dudley, went off to the Holy Land to do battle and did not return for several years. She, thinking him dead, built a little cell on Bury Hill and devoted her life to helping the poor. In the end, Ralph did return, they married and lived happily ever after. The legend tells us that the Lady Brade was "of form as slight as a mountain deer, and shyly from her veiled hood, her golden tresses forth did peer, bright as the sunbeams through the wood".
A legend; a local fairy tale or, did the golden haired lass really exist?

But it is to reminisce that I must return and see the beauty of Bury Hill.
Through adolescent eyes it was a mountain. It was the home not only of ferocious wild animals, trolls, goblins and witches but of all things that decidedly go bump in the night. It was a place of wild beauty. Not for Bury Hill a mantle of pampered turf with little notices threatening dire consequences if one dared to place a footprint on its coiffured sward. Like the people it watches over, the hill wears its overalls with pride. Tough grass that can take a pounding from countless pairs of feet and, in those far off winters, provided a surface for the best sledging in the world if not, (in those impressionable years) the universe.

And, when the world crashed around young ears, one could climb to the quietness of its summit and sit with only nature as a companion. Below, the town stretched out to the horizon, and one strained one's eyes to pinpoint the street, or even the very house, where one lived. Caught up in the conglomeration of broken down houses, noisy factories and belching chimney stacks, the world had seemed an indifferent place to a young boy. Now, one was above it; one had left that place of mortals to walk Olympian heights where troubled thoughts are banished by a stiffening breeze of linnets' song. One gazed at the town with renewed vision and streets, an hour since threatening, became homely, and safe, filled with food, friends and caring family. That is the power of beauty.

To some people, Bury Hill might only be a lump of rock of geological interest. To others, a mystical piece of legend, folklore and an unbreakable bond with antiquity. Most, I suppose, never even give it a second glance. But, for me it is a green, fresh patch that gently dominates the town in which I live. An inextricable part of my life. Just one of the many small, but thriving oases that go to make up the beautiful Black Country.

Brian Counley is a professional writer living in Oldbury.
The above is an extract from the forthcoming book "The Beautiful Black Country" .

SAINT BRADE AND OTHER LEGENDS

The legend of St Brade is by far the best known of the folklore of Oldbury, being immortalised in verse by the Rev. Arthur W. Fox M.A., on a visit to Oldbury from Christ College, Cambridge. The ballad is narrated by one Gwyllim of Duddeley, a monk. It begins:

> In auncient dayes there dwelled a maide,
> In Burye's mullioned Castell Hall;
> Y-cleped was shee, the Ladie Brade,
> Whose pitteous hart would bleed for all.

St Brade of Bury Castle is recognisable as the daughter of Roger de Mortuomari (Mortimer), sheriff of Shropshire, who had charge of Hales Regis, of which Oldbury was a part during the reign of Richard the First. She became betrothed to the heir to Dudley, Ralph de Somery, who sailed to Palestine in 1195, probably as a 'free lance' or in the train of a German Prince. Although this crusade ended in 1196 he did not return home at once. His isolation as an Englishman among foreigners may have separated him from their company and sympathy, and in wanderings and perhaps imprisonments the years fled by. The Lady Brade was to

8

remain with her father until Ralph's return, but as the years passed she finally gave him up for lost and took up permanent abode at Bury, resolving to devote herself to charitable endeavours. The well there, like the well of Holy Cross (Crosswell) was celebrated for its healing virtues, as was the stream of Holy Rood (Rood End), and pilgrims came from far to drink of these waters. Brade determined to build a shrine and shelter for these poor and distressed travellers. She also erected a little cell for herself and lived there as a hermit. On one of her frequent walks to Dudley Priory to visit her relative, the aged Prior, she fell in with a Palmer (a pilgrim bearing a palm branch as a sign of a visit to the Holy Land), who proved to be her betrothed in disguise, returned home hale and sound to claim his bride.

Reference to another local folk tale appears in the poem 'Barnford Hill', by T. Wilks, the line "If some lone sound was heard around" can be found. McKean, writing in 1900, tells us that "more than twenty years ago a legend appeared in the 'Post' or 'Journal' (I forget which) anent a blacksmith being heard blowing his fire underneath Barnford Hill".

BARNFORD HILL *J. Beete Jukes*

The Permean Calcareous Conglomerate is well shown at Barnford Hill, two miles South of Oldbury, and thence to Brand Hall. It is composed almost entirely of rounded and semi-rounded fragments of mountain limestone and chert. It is about twenty feet thick, and is in several places quarried and the limestone pebbles burnt for lime.

from "South Staffordshire Coalfield (2nd edition)".

BURY CASTLE *Treadway Russell Nash*

No vestiges of this sort (camp or barrow) appear now at Oldbury, but a very aged inhabitant informed me that in his father's time there were apparent ruins of a town near a certain pasture called the Castle Leasow, and that a castle was said to have stood at the lower end of the said leasow, near the Well-hill. He added that a causeway still remains in the lands of one Harold, directly leading to the Castle Leasow. In confirmation of this, I find a general tradition among the inhabitants that a great town anciently stood here, which extended from the present village to the Castle Leasow, lying under the Bury Hill, which is near half a mile.

from "Nash's Worcestershire".

A TONGUE OF WIGORNIAN TERRITORY

Frederick William Hackwood

Oldbury is a township which never was a parish - that is, in the legal sense that it was an area of civil administration imposed on an ancient ecclesiastical foundation.

When the English Constitution was taking root in the land, and the old form of tribal government was waning before the dawn of Christianity and the domination of clericalism which accompanied it, the country was gradually divided into dioceses by the missioner bishops, who presently, having quite dispelled the mists of paganism, organised their sees into local government units called parishes. Oldbury was then, and for a long time afterwards, included in the parish of Halesowen.

Now it is nearly always possible to dig out the history of a parish from the various ancient parochial records; but a fraction of a parish, which was not always a separate entity, the task is by no means so easy. The first constitution of Oldbury into a distinct entity came at a later period, when its area was organised for civil and military government into a feudal manor. But, unfortunately, few of the old manorial records have survived, and again the historian is at a loss.

To complicate matters still more the mother-parish, Halesowen, was not always included, for its wider government and superior civic administration, within the County of Worcester, to which it geographically belongs, but formed for several centuries a detached and outlying portion of Shropshire.

Nor was the whole of Halesowen included in Salop. It is a large parish of several townships, one of which was already in Worcestershire, as is testified by its name, Warley Wigorn. And it did not consist of one piece; it was cut up into small patches and scattered among the townships of Oldbury, Langley, and Warley Salop, which were in Shropshire, so that on the small scale ordnance maps it was scarcely possible to distinguish the boundaries of the two counties. These anomalous dislocations and confusing boundary lines, after existing for centuries, were rectified by statute a few years after the passing of the great Reform Bill of 1832.

And when this detached piece of Shropshire was eventually taken into Worcestershire, it formed a tongue of Wigornian territory, which thrust itself like a peninsula of foreign soil into Staffordshire - an intrusion which the precisians said ought to be rectified by merging it into that county.

So a movement was set on foot for transferring Oldbury from Worcestershire to Staffordshire. At the reform of the Poor Laws in 1834, Oldbury, for some occult reason or other, had been included in the Poor Law Union of West Bromwich, an important administrative area on which the Local Government Board focussed all its official papers, so that for years and years this poor little slice of Worcestershire was administered and overshadowed in a government unit that comprised a wide area of Staffordshire parishes - West Bromwich, Wednesbury, and Handsworth.

The promoters of the movement for transference urged that Oldbury was already in the West Bromwich Union, and that on three sides out of four it was hemmed in by Smethwick, West Bromwich, and Rowley, all Staffordshire areas. The Oldbury governing authorities, however, resisted the proposed transfer, feeling that it was in every way preferable to remain one of the larger towns of Worcestershire, than to be tacked on to one of the great urban districts of populous Staffordshire.

An opportunity to revive the project occurred in 1906, when Oldbury joined with Smethwick in a scheme for the provision of a joint Infectious Hospital. This time strong opposition was offered by the Worcester County Council, which naturally objected to losing one of its most important industrial towns, which was the centre of one of its largest Parliamentary divisions, and which comprised a rateable area of considerable value in a county so largely agricultural.

Market Place OLDBURY

Published by Roden & Son, Church St., Oldbury.

Market Place, Oldbury.
From a postcard published by Roden & Son (see Pg. 36).

The proposal was not allowed to die. Public movements fanned it into life at various times; as when Smethwick was constituted a county borough, and again when the development of the Black Country tramway system linked it up into closer communication with the adjacent Staffordshire towns. It almost seemed to onlookers at these contentions that the rights of self government in the township might be invaded, if not denied, and the place regarded merely as a prize for which two powerful bodies might contend at will, without any reference to the wishes of the inhabitants themselves.

How was it that this outlying portion of Halesowen should have developed into a busy industrial centre, while the heart of that ancient parish scarcely outgrew its pristine rurality? The reason is not far to seek. Oldbury not only possessed great mineral resources, but when the period of industrialism first dawned it was found on the important coach road between Birmingham and Shrewsbury and the north.

The "Britannia Depicta", published in 1753, says that the old road from Birmingham via Dudley and Bridgnorth "is now disused" by the coaches and wagons, and goes on to recommend the newer and better road through West Bromwich, Wednesbury, and Wolverhampton, which was turnpiked in 1721.
This, however, is evidently a quotation from "Owen and Bowen's Road Book," published in 1731, containing the earliest mention of these local highways.

Far more ancient than the recommended road from Birmingham leading to the north and north-west through Sandwell and West Bromwich, is that connecting Birmingham with Dudley and its dependencies, going through Oldbury, or by the still more direct line passing a little to the right of Rowley Regis, which gives evidence by its "hollowed ways" of having been used for regular traffic at a very remote period. Oakham, it may be noted, was originally "Hollow-combe."

Probably the oldest coach route in this direction lay through Oldbury,Dudley and Wenlock. Daily postal communication between Birmingham and Dudley, Halesowen, Stourbridge, Kidderminster, and Bewdley was first established in 1769.

In passing through Oldbury a century ago, the traveller obtained a fine view of the surrounding country - of the Rowley Hills, the ruins of Dudley Castle, and the fine woods of Sandwell Park. But the pristine rusticity of the place was beginning to fade.

The road from Birmingham to Dudley through Oldbury is about nine miles, or nearly a mile shorter than the one through West Bromwich, Carter's Green, and Great Bridge. Yet in that short space, the traveller formerly passed through four different counties; Birmingham being in Warwickshire, Smethwick in Staffordshire, Oldbury in Shropshire and Dudley in Worcestershire. The eccentricity and arbitrariness of English political boundaries could scarcely further go than this.

Another stimulus to the growth of Oldbury was given in the latter half of the eighteenth century by the construction of artificial waterways in this high midland region where navigable rivers are unknown. When the rapidly growing traffic in coal, iron, and other heavy produce first called into being the canals, it was a fortunate thing for Oldbury that the new waterway between Birmingham and the ancient coalfield in the heart of the Black Country - the original mining region round Wednesbury, Bilston, and Sedgley - ran directly through this developing township. Though the canals came first in 1769, a decade or two elapsed before they had their inevitable effect on the development of this fortunately situated village.

from "Oldbury and Round About", 1915.

ON THE MAP: THE NEW OLDBURY   *Henry McKean*

The Oldbury embraced by the Urban District Council of Oldbury comprises the townships of Oldbury and Langley and the Parish of Warley. The district is bounded by Birmingham, Smethwick, West Bromwich, Rowley Regis, Cakemore, Quinton, and Ridgeacre, and contains 3548 acres. The map of 1857 will give an idea of ancient Oldbury and Langley, but, subsequently, all the outlying and isolated portions were handed over to Langley. The story of these isolated parts of Oldbury, Langley, and Warley will perhaps never be known, but it must be one of love or war, of marriage portions, of fights for a habitation and a home in a neighbour's territory. The Oldbury portions all came back to their old home on the formation of the new Oldbury in 1894.

There is a tradition that only one man ever succeeded in mastering the old boundaries and the effort was so great that he died.

from "Picturesque Oldbury" 1900.

ON THE ROAD FROM BIRMINGHAM TO SMETHWICK

Charles Pye

"Leaving Smethwick, you proceed towards Oldbury, upon which road the trustees are making great improvements, by widening the road and turning the course of a brook, over which they are building a bridge, which, when finished, will be a great accommodation. This village is situated in the County of Salop, and is a chapel-of-ease to Halesowen.

from "Modern Birmingham," written in 1829.

LEAVING BIRMINGHAM

Walter White

"We now start for another walk, journeying the first few miles by railway. The Stour Valley line accompanies for some distance the broad canal - one of Telford's latest works, which runs the whole length of the Black Country without a lock, contrasting with the crookedness of Brindley's canal adjoining. Soon we are speeding past Soho, and great heaps of coal, coke, and clinkers, great refuse heaps that look like waste mortar; past large patches of wild camomile, and here and there potato patches, and little venturesome gardens that tempt Nature under very discouraging circumstances. The temptation is not in vain; for the flowers and vegetables do grow, and station walls look gay with nasturtiums. We alight at Oldbury, in Worcestershire, a place of smother amid smother, and , on leaving the station, can count seventy-nine furnace and factory chimneys without turning round, all of which pour forth their cloudy contributions, varied by the blue and yellow smoke of copper-works, while noises resound afar. Among the chimneys rise those of a phosphorus factory, where, with some risk, and in a fierce temperature, phosphorus is extracted from bones, in such quantities that England, which used to import now exports the article, sending many tons to Vienna, and receiving it back on the ends of matches by hundreds of millions every week. One pound of phosphorus, worth about two-and-ninepence, suffices to charge a million matches.

While we walk through the shabby-looking town, Temperans tells me, that, not till recently, when a public meeting was held to start a savings bank, could working men find a single place in Oldbury to help them to save money, although there were two hundred public-houses to entice them to spend it. He had to follow a speaker at the meeting who held up riches and greatness as the objects most worthy of pursuit; and, taking a truer view, impressed the crowd of hard-handed listeners

14

with his conviction that goodness would prove to be a more satisfactory prize than either. Here, as elsewhere, are signs of plenty to eat; piles of wheaten bread, such as German artisans never see, unless a Serene Highness invites them to breakfast; and the stores of drapery are suggestive of plenty to wear. A man shows us the 'gainest way' to our destination, and corrects himself with 'You'll do't more gain'; and reminds us of the dialect of Mercia. 'Hur's naish enough for a leddy,' said a miner, speaking of his wife one day to Temperans, meaning that she was very finical; and another described his wife as the 'esfosterinist woman as ever was.' What did he mean?

Presently we come to clay-diggings, and more patches of wild camomile and clover, and docks and coltsfoot, and here and there dead trees, and such ragged, perishing hedgerows as are pitiable to look on with the thought that they once looked beautiful and smelt sweetly with the bloom of May. Then appears an ironstone pit, with little tramways, and not far off, a characteristic sign, the Whimsey Inn. Then we see - a frequent sight in the Black Country - houses hooped with iron to keep them from tumbling to pieces. The ground is so widely undermined that sinkings continually occur, to the detriment of all that stands on the surface, and you can hardly see a perpendicular chimney or house; and in some instances the distortion is so great that fall seems imminent.
(Temperans is a lay figure upon whom White hangs his moralisings).

from "All Around the Wrekin" a walking tour of the Midlands (1860).

A WALK AROUND OLDBURY 1993
Quotes by members of Simpson Street Day Centre during a walk around Oldbury.

" With the old Town Hall we've got a lovely old building that's been renovated and just in front of it you've got an old telephone box which for the want of a lick of paint and a couple of hundred pound being spent on it could blend in with the building. Give it more of a 'period' feel. And you've got these Belisha beacons which you don't see very often and I hope that these are kept as well."

" I quite like the new Council House. I think it's worth all the money that's been spent on it. It reminds me of the Hanging Gardens of Babylon, at least it would if they put a few flower boxes on it - trailing plants coming down..."

" I don't like the Council House, I think it looks too new for Oldbury. In my mind Oldbury is still an old town, a Victorian town - even the name lends itself to that image: Old-bury." 15

Corporation Refuse Truck No. 2.

TRUCK NUMBER 2 *Alf Parkes*

I drove the Corporation Refuse Truck for 40 years from the time that I returned
from Egypt in 1942. The first truck that we had, No 1, had solid tyres. No 2 had
pneumatic tyres but it was still like driving a tram. It had no steering wheel - you
had to sit in the centre of the cab and operate a handle on your right hand side to
steer with and a gear change on your left. There was one seat for a passenger
which had to be folded down. Both of the trucks were made by a company called
Shelvoke and Drury.

We started work at 7 am and worked through until 5 pm, having to take a proper
breakfast and lunch break - we weren't allowed to work straight through until we'd
finished our work in those days. We also had to work on Saturday mornings.
Although we were later issued with protective clothing, when I first started in 1942
we had to work in our own clothes and even find our own gloves - we used to wear
old socks, or anything, to protect our hands. It was hard work then because it was
all bins, not plastic sacks, and they would all have ashes in them, making them
quite heavy.

MILESTONES   *Alex Hadley*

"Now ar've bin a stondin 'ear fa lunger thun ar care to remember. The day ar was put onta the cart number 110 sid tha' ar would be put inta a field miles frum any weer. But ar day believe tha', not afta o'd Jack 'ad spent two months chippin me out. But he wer right, well almust.

When tha' lad tuc off the tarpalin ar tried ta tell 'em abart me left footin, but 'e day tec a blind bit ov notice. Ar knew tha' the wairter would get in. On ar cursed 'em fa mower thun sixty 'ears, with all manor ov things that ar'd do to him. Then one day 'e cum back. 'E wur gray and o'd, but ar knew from outa u'l the 'onds tha' 'ad touched me over the 'ears tha' it wur 'em. 'E touched me an sid, 'Ya still ear then o'd mon', an 'e walked off with a limp. Meby 'e wur suffrin as much as ar'v bin.

Ar cur mowon though, 'e put me in a nice enough place. Frum wer ar stood, ar bet ya as I cod see down inta Wales an up inta Stafferd. Fields an trees fa as far as ya eye cod see. Now tha' wur Englands green an pleasant land.

Frum weer ar stond, ya cod've sin it all grow. Down the illside they cum, rows an rows ov back ta back 'ouses. Whums fa the workers tha' dug out the cuts, whums fa the colliers, chainmekers an nailmekers. Ar cod see foundries an steel works, coal mines an' brick yards, glass an pipe works, gas works an goods yards; mekin an shippin goods ta all parts ov the world.

Ya ar watched it all grow. Now there wur times tha' I couldn't see anythin, couse ov the fog. 'Pasoupers' is what we called 'um. Tha wus when the low cloud got stuck under the smoke frum the chimney stacks. The've bin known ta last fa days.

The towns growd up around me now, an ar cor see mowerun sixty yards in each way. It ta all tha' bad stondin 'ere. Ar like ta see folk apassin by. Ar try ta listern ta wot they bin asayin. Like the time ov the Royol Visit. Ar got a new coat ov paint fa tha'. They cleaned up the o'd place from top ta bottum. Hung out flags an buntin. Now me footins are almust three foot deep, but yo cod ov nocked me down weth a feather, after wot ar'd 'eard.

O'd Queen Victoria 'ad bin advised ta keep 'er winda blind down as not ta see the bad state the place wur in. Now tha' cut deep tha' did. When ya think ov all the thins tha' cum frum the Black Country ta help build 'er Empire. Well we wo goo into tha' now.

The new Queen's visit wus another matter. Not ony did she kep 'er winda blind up, but she aven got out an shook 'onds weth the mayor. Pity o'd Polly wur 'ere ta see it. 'Er bin so proad. Why folk called 'er 'Polly on the Fountain' ar dow know. 'Er real nerm wur 'Europe'. Ar bet 'er could tell ya a thing or two abart changes. She stood fa over sixty 'ears, outside ov Lloyds Bonk.

Ar the Bonk. Now tha's sumert ta talk abart. Did yo know tha' it wus the fust bonk tha' Lloyds opened outsida ov Brum. Albright un Wilson Ltd kept 'avin their wages pinched when they tried ta move um frum Brum ta the works. So they talked Lloyds inta opening a new branch. Tha wus back in 1864. The bonk wus good fa the market an a'l. Folks ud cum frum miles around to do their shoppin 'ere. There wus a sayin tha' went, 'If yo cor buy it at Oldbury, ya cor buy it at all'.

Polly cum 'ere in 1882. 'Er wus a drinkin fontin for 'oses. She were a welcum sight for many a tired 'ose, un mon fa tha' matter. Yo cod see the 'orses start ta pick up speed when they sin 'er stondin proad, 'oldin 'er torch up 'igh. Now 'er's gone. Afta sixty sevan 'ears: two World Wars un the Great Depression.

Ar it wus Christmas eve ov 1949, ar con remember it like it were yesterde. They cum outa the o'd pub, as drunk as Lords the'd bin. An one on um decides ta give o'd Polly a kiss fa Christmas. Up 'e climbed. Then 'e begun ta do a jig. Well are Polly wus a lady, un she wur 'avin none a tha'. Down 'er cum, crashin ta the ground. She wus med outa cast iron ya know. Well 'er arm got broke ov. They kept 'er in the library fa a bit, then 'er was moved off ta Wiltshire, we're eva tha' is. Ar'v 'erd that' they tr'in ta get 'er back. Ar hope they do, ar'd like ta see 'er agin.

There wus this o'd mon, 'ed goo around aselin lomp oil. 'E 'ad an 'ose an cart wuth a tonk on it. 'E'd serve folks frum a tap. Every other night, 'ed cum up the street, tie 'is 'ose up wuth Polly, an befowa 'ed get ta the pub, this kid would run ta 'im an say, 'Watch ya 'ose fa a penny Mr'. 'Ar OK', 'e'd say, 'Now dow ya pinch any, ar know how much the're is in it'. No soona wus tha' mon inta the pub, the kid would tec out a bottle an fill it wuth lomp oil. Then e'd hide it behind we. Many a time ar saw tha' o'd mon a lookin out tha winda, watchin the lad nick 'is oil, but 'e never sid a werd, an e'd allwis pay the lad 'is penny. Now it's all tha' electric light. Sum folks we're afeared ov it, an day 'ave it in ther 'ouse, nor gas. They did the cookin on the stove an lit up the 'ouse wuth condles or lomps.

Ar con remember when this street was fula life. Tec Adams the drapers. Ar watched 'is business grow frum a small shop ta become the biggest in the town. But tha' 'adta close down afta nearly eighty 'ears.

18

Ar dow see any we're near the folks tha' ar use ta. The buses dow cum up 'ere anymower. Ar con just mek out the road down the bonk. They've med it wider now. Ar con remember when it was just a dirt track. Now the cars goo a speedin, around the back ov me. They oney cum up 'ere when they wont ta get out ov a traffic jam.

The market is so small that nobody knows it's there. But ar think tha' there is mower people here than ar con see. Ar con feel um through me bad footin. Ar think it's sumthin ta do wuth all tha' construction tha' wur agooin on a few 'ears back. But tha's OK, a few 'ears ov peace un quiet will do me good. Things will change, the alwiz do. So until then ar kep on doin me job, just like ar'v allwis done.

I up, 'ere cums sumbody now. Ya 'is gooin ta 'ave a look. Ar tha's right mate. London 114 miles, B'ham 5 miles, an Dudley 3 miles the other road".

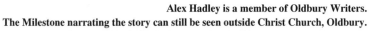

Alex Hadley is a member of Oldbury Writers.
The Milestone narrating the story can still be seen outside Christ Church, Oldbury.

Polly on the Fountain.

'Polly on the Fountain' - The statue's actual name was 'Europe'. It stood in Oldbury until it was removed after being damaged by revellers on Christmas Eve 1949. It was given to descendants of David Taylor, founder of the London Iron-works, who had donated it to the town in 1882. Mr and Mrs Nightingale took it to Wiltshire where they went to live. It was agreed to return Polly to the area, but The Warley News Telephone, Thurs 8th January 1970, reported that the it would cost £300 to repair it. Cllr. Fletcher said, "The estimate is really too much to spend on a statue, even if it does have sentimental value". Polly was eventually returned to the South of England.

19

THE BRADES 1829 *Charles Pye*

"The Protestant Dissenters have here a neat place of worship, as have also the Methodists.

"Close to the village are several coal mines, and a blast furnace belonging to Mr. Parker.

"About a mile distant, on the left of the road, is the Brades, where Messrs. William Hunt and Sons have established a manufacture of iron and steel, which they form into scythes, hay knives, trowels, and every kind of hoe now in use."

IT'S TOUGH DOWN THE BRADES *Wilf Carter*

There was a song that they used to sing about the Brades Company in Brades Road:

> "It's tough, mighty tough, down the Brades,
> They make all the pecks and the shovels and spades".

And they did, they made spades, trowels, axes: every tool. Their sports pavilion was where the Dayla building stands now.

A THREE-LEGGED TROWEL *Brian Counley*

Black Countrymen have, (and still do) made the best edge tools in the world, for example; from stainless steel spades and forks used by the 'more discerning' gardener, to machetes, adzes and great hefty chopping hoes still in use in Third World countries. Brades, Skelton and Tyzack included such tools in its catalogue, along with builders tools which became famous throughout the world for their quality. Craftsmen builders asked for the very best in tools and their favourites were those bearing the three legged trade mark of Tyzack. They never asked the ironmonger for a 'Tyzack' trowel; it was always a 'three-legged' trowel.

Brades, however, had made its name long before that. They were regarded as the country's foremost manufacturer of ramrods used in charging firearms carried by Britain's armed forces during the Napoleonic Wars. Takeovers and amalgamations during more recent times resulted in the company being lost in that conglomeration of other edge tool firms that now goes to make up Spear and Jackson Garden Tools Ltd., based at Wednesbury.

20

FISH IN THE TROUBLED FOUNTAIN…The Bromford Works
Elihu Burritt

"Not far from the Brades works are the Bromford works of the Messrs. Dawes, perhaps equally celebrated for the production of the best kind of iron bar. Indeed, they may be regarded as a representative establishment of the district; and I visited them one day with peculiar interest. When in full operation, with their sixty puddling furnaces in action, they present a scene which would have stirred the muse of Homer or Virgil beyond any of their vivid fancies. Puddles! Mud puddles! What rustic Saxon similes are applied to these fierce operations! To an outsider looking into one of those sixty furnaces, and seeing, if his eyes would bear it, the boiling, bubbling mass of metal, ten times more than red hot, a puddle would sound too wet and watery to describe it. The puddlers who fish in the troubled fountain are generally stripped to the waist, and flooded with perspiration. They fish out a mass at the end of the rod, of a weight which shows what athletes they are trained to be. I hardly know what figure to use to convey an idea of the appearance and consistency of this burning, frittering, fizzy mass of metal thus brought out of the furnace. Should one dip a large sponge into a mud puddle it would fill in a moment with the impure matter, which, on compression, would all flow out again, leaving the sponge as it was before the dip. There is this difference in the simile: the meshes of the sponge are in the metal puddle itself, and they all come together with the mass. This mass, cooling a little on its way to make it more coherent, goes under a hammer, or into a squeezing machine, which, at the first blow or turn, throws out the spray of the impure puddle-matter, such as melted stone, cinder, etc. Thus the sponge part is only the genuine iron meshes or grains, which are thus squeezed and hammered and rolled into solid bars. To see these masses at white heat running down iron slideways from every direction to the squeezers, hammers, and rollers, is a stirring sight. Some of these hammers are of tremendous power, especially the Nasmyth pounder. When it falls with a ton weight upon a liquid boulder, you will see a horizontal shower of meteors, which would penetrate a suit of the best broadcloth at a considerable distance. There was a machine called the squeezer which operated to admiration in the first stages. It was a large fluted horizontal wheel which turned in a fluted semi-circular case, the receiving being twice as large as the delivering hopper. A mass of the half-liquid material was thrust in on the left, and pressed into a constantly narrowing space, until it was delivered, at the right, a compact elongated roll ready for the trip-hammer or rolling machine."

Elihu Burritt was U.S. Consul to Birmingham and wrote 'Walks in The Black Country' (1868).

PUDDLING FURNACES   *Frederick William Hackwood*

Of puddling furnaces in Oldbury there were (in 1873) 69 at Bromford, 13 at
Brittains, 12 at The Brades, and 10 at the Eagle works of Messrs. Simpson; while
beyond, on one side of the town there were quite a hundred at Smethwick, and at
Tipton on the other side there were the same number at one works alone (that of
Messrs. Barrows).

It was indeed a region of furnaces, ovens, and kilns; of forges, factories, and iron-
mills; the dull and depressing landscape varied only by heaps of cinder, slag, or
miniature mountains of pit refuse, and relieved but slightly, if at all, by intersecting
canals that appeared to be fed by water of the colour and consistency of pea-soup,
and which indeed, near to the great furnaces, sometimes steamed like that nourish-
ing compound.

At night the sky was illuminated by the lurid glare of the countless furnaces,
varying in shade from the blood-red flame of the puddling furnace to the streaked
white and red of the blast-furnace, and diversified here by the yellow and blue
flames of the copper works. By day dense clouds of smoke obscured the light of
heaven, and kept off the vivifying rays of the sun with destructive effects to the
struggling vegetation. Corroding gases emitted from chemical works in the heart
of the town so completed the blight that even grass and the hardiest of plants failed
not to succumb in due time. Not by incessant labour could Oldbury housewives
keep fire-irons or other household utensils of bright steel in any desirable condition
of cleanliness; metal tarnished in a single night, and in the process of time slowly
corroded away as they had been petals of a fading flower.

THE TOWN OF THE FOUR MOONS   *Alfred R. R. Bennett*

"... the powers-that-be resisted many attempts to have the town lit by gaslight in the early
19th century. The reason for this was that at this time there were a number of blast furnaces
in the town, four of which were so bright that they gave a better light than any gas lamp. So
Oldbury earned for itself the title of the 'town of the four moons'." John Richards. West
Bromwich Mail, Friday September 10, 1971.

The tops of the blast furnaces were covered by a domed circular lid or cover
known as the 'cupola'. When it was raised to drop a load of material down into the
blazing hot furnace, the interior glare and sparks lit up the sky and was reflected
back from the underside of the clouds to bathe the area in its radiant glow. When 1,
2, 3 and 4 furnaces opened up at the same time there was a much appreciated 'Four
Moons' aspect - and at no extra charge on the town rates!

Yet long before Oldbury was given this notable title the people of this area, and in many parts of the Black Country, referred to the moon, especially when at 'full moon' as their 'cottage lantern'.

Even children had their own description of the moonlight effect with their song "Boys and girls come out to play, the moon doth shine as bright as day". I well remember that in 1939 I myself worked 'overtime' digging a hole deep enough for a 6' x 4' Anderson Shelter by bright moonlight because of being at work all day.

Alfred R.R. Bennett lives in Oldbury.

"MADE IN OLDBURY" - 1949

Even Beyond the Lost Horizon they knew of Oldbury.

Just before the war, an expedition exploring New Guinea crossed a mountain range never before climbed. On the other side they found a great valley where lived a tribe of people who had never had any contact with the outside world, a tribe who believed the earth only extended to the mountain ridge they had never seen beyond, and who thought they were the only people who existed. yet that tribe had one very proud possession - a hunting knife made in Oldbury. How it got there has never been explained.

That true story is a good introduction to Oldbury's industry, because you cannot go anywhere in the world without finding products made in Oldbury. Oldbury is a small town, with only 53,000 population. It has no imposing civic buildings, no big shopping centre, and much of it, to be honest, is rather dirty. But it's honest dirt - the dirt that comes from a hard day's work, not from slovenliness. For when it comes to industry, this small town of Oldbury can hold its own with any other town or city in the world.

Back in 1769 Oldbury looked very different, a collection of scattered villages and farms adding up to less than a thousand people. The group of forges which later became the Brades were working, and other forges made nails and similar smallwares - only goods small in size and weight could be carried out along the roads which were often inches deep in mud. But 1769 was an important year in Oldbury's history, for it was then that the first canal was cut through the town. The new and cheap method of transporting heavy goods at once opened up Oldbury's possibilities as an industrial centre. the iron and the coal were there, so was the clay for the bricks. Coal mines, blast furnaces and brickyards were founded - industries which relied on cheap transport, and which could never have flourished in the days when the horse wagon was the only method of moving goods from place to place.

The canal system, throwing out its arms to meet the needs of Oldbury's expanding industry, grew into the complex network which today makes an island of the town centre. For nearly a hundred years these canals carried the traffic to and from Oldbury - traffic which was not only industrial, but tourist as well. In 1839, for instance, the members of the British Association travelled by canal through Oldbury to see the Dudley caverns, lit for the occasion by 1,600 dozen candles. The story has it that the boat's manifest was made out to read: "Draught, 13 inches; weight 3 1/4 tons; cargo, philosophers."

One example of local industrial initiative over a century ago is well worth noting - the invention by an Oldbury man, Cornelius Whitehouse, of the lap-welded tube. Whitehouse's invention, in 1825, speeded up the introduction of coal gas lighting, at that time held up for lack of cheap tubing, but he could have had little idea of Oldbury's great tube industry of today.

The chemical industry came to Oldbury in 1835, when Chance Brothers set up a plant for making raw materials needed at their Spon Lane glassworks. That was the works which later became Chance and Hunt, and it was followed by Albright and Wilson, who moved to Oldbury in the 1850's to be near their raw material supplies. In 1865 the Demuth Tar Works were built to give chemicals an even more important place on the Oldbury Map.

Oldbury has not only been delivering the goods, but it has carried out repairs and extensions under full steam. "Made in Oldbury" will be a phrase known even more widely, in the future, than in the past.

An extract from introduction to the catalogue for 'Made in Oldbury' an Exhibition of Local Industrial Effort held at Langley Baths, March 30th - April 2nd, 1949.

*Case of 8050 pieces of Drawn Seamless Tube from the stock of Accles and Pollock
exhibited at World's Fair New York 1939.*

PUTTING THE METAL ROUND HOLES

In 1899, in Perry Barr, the Accles Tube Syndicate was renting a tubemill from the
official receiver. Holford Mill, under the name of Accles Ltd., had been set up by
George Accles, a brilliant American engineer and perfector of the Gatling gun, to
exploit the relatively new process of of cold drawing with its considerable poten-
tial in the booming bicycle industry. The company met financial difficulties and it
was George Accles' secretary, Charles Barlow, who eventually set up the

25

firm which was to become Accles & Pollock. No sooner had the new company begun trading than they were given notice to quit Holford Mill. The only feasible alternative was a dilapidated shed a few miles away in Oldbury.

Accles & Pollock's first foreman, who rose to be managing director, then chairman, and in retirement, president of the company, was Walter William Hackett CBE, JP; born 1874 died 1964. His inventiveness in the art of tubemaking was matched only by his flair for recollecting Black Country anecdotes and committing some to verse under his pen name of Khanyer Whackett.

On the move to Oldbury he said: "The first time I saw it was on the 3rd February 1902. It was a snow storm. The mill was only partly enclosed. There was hardly a window that was not broken. My first impression was BB - B means bad ..... There were only twenty of us came from Holford and I wondered would they stay. The friendly natives encouraged us. They told how it had been a foundry, a glass factory, a nail factory, a copper tube drawing factory - all these had been and nobody had done any good there; they had all failed. Oh it did cheer us ... but the men did stay. They worked well and happily and I often think, looking back, that it was the sense of humour they possessed that helped to carry us through a very trying time under very trying conditions."

With the outbreak of the First World War, Accles & Pollock, as the only company producing tubes for aircraft, was put under government control. Hackett had many tales to tell of the Man from the Ministry's visits to Oldbury. One such involved explaining how tubes were made in response to the official's query:
"He said, 'Let me see, what do you make?'
And I said, 'We make tubes.'
'Ah, it's wonderful how tubes are made,' he said. 'Do you know that I went to a place last week and saw a white hot billet of steel go into a machine and come out a tube.'
'Oh no,' I said, 'That's not the way we do it here.'
He said, 'How do you do it?'
I said, 'Well look here, if you come to us for a 2 and a half inch tube with a 2 inch hole we'd take a 2 inch hole and put quarter inch metal all the way round it. Then you'd have 2 inches plus two quarter inches - that's 2 and a half inch tube.'
'Oh I see, I see.'
It was going alright when Charlie Barlow burst out laughing and that made it a bit awkward for me ...."

from "Accles & Pollock 1899-1974: The First Seventy Five Years of Achievement".

THE OLDBURY MINING DISTRICT

Frederick William Hackwood

Oldbury, like Dudley, is a Worcestershire town falling within the benign influences of the prosperous South Staffordshire Coalfield.

Good coal and plenty of it existed at Oldbury, and the new canals found a good and ready market for it, speedily developing the place into a thriving colliery region. By the middle of the nineteenth century Oldbury had all the industrial and social characteristics that had belonged to Wednesbury and Bilston and the older parts of the coalfield for a century or so.

Even with the advances made in the methods of working the seam, the coal-mining of Oldbury was not free from the usual toll on the lives of the colliers, and one fatal accident in the July of 1866 raised a legal question of some importance at the time. The Mines Inspection Act of 1860 required that places which were suspected of being foul, though they were not in actual working, should be fenced off so as to prevent any person going into them. At the Bromford Colliery of Mr. W. H. Dawes was an old gate-road, which was known to contain choke damp, yet was not properly fenced off. Three pit boys walked into it, and were suffocated. Then the question of responsibility was raised. Did it lie with the owner, Mr. Dawes, or with the Charter-master? When Mr. J. Cope was proceeded against he pleaded that he was Consulting Mining Agent, and not an agent responsible according to the provisions of the Mines Inspection Act. The Stipendiary Magistrate, however, decided that he was the responsible person under the Act. The effect of the decision was to make any Consulting Mining Agent, or Engineer, responsible for the safe working of any mine in connection with which he gave professional advice or assistance.

On November 9th, 1846, a very serious fire-damp explosion occurred at Rounds Green Colliery, concerning which Mr. Smyth was appointed by the Home Secretary to hold an inquiry. His report showed that no efficient system of ventilation had been employed at the colliery. Consequently large quantities of fire-damp accumulated in these old workings, and often found their way into the gate-roads. The outcome of this enquiry was the submission of Mr. Smyth's report to two expert scientists, Sir H. T. De la Beche and Dr. Lyon Playfair, who had no hesitation in advising the authorities that such a condition of things called for the establishment of a government system of mine inspection.

Strangely enough, soon after, when the first Act for the inspection of coal mines had been passed, a disastrous explosion occurred at the Ramrod Hall Colliery; this was on August 13th, 1856, and eleven lives were lost. In this case the pit had been idle for four days; again the shafts were about equal in length, and there was no furnace to assist the ventilation. The Charter-master, or "butty", being anxious to resume working as quickly as possible, and regardless of warm weather and a low barometer, sent down eight men without making any preliminary examination for the fire-damp which was almost sure to have accumulated. The men detected the gas immediately they reached the bottom, and signalled for a lighted safety lamp to be sent down. Instead of complying, the "butty" himself got into the skip, along with seven more men, taking a shovelful of fire with them, and they had not descended twenty yards before, naturally enough, a tremendous explosion occurred. All the eight men in the skip lost their lives, as well as three of the others at the bottom of the shaft. The fatuity of the old-time butty-collier was responsible for countless "accidents" of this type.

Another type of accident, not infrequent in those days of the "rule of thumb", was the boiler explosion, which, in connection with colliery winding or pumping engines, was doubly disastrous. One such fatal explosion occurred to a much-worn balloon boiler at Rounds Green Colliery in the March of 1857; and another to a cylindrical boiler of good plates, usually working at 40 lbs to the square inch, occurred in the following December at Bullocks Farm Colliery, Spon Lane.

In the old colliery life of the Black Country there were often economic troubles as well as mechanical disasters. In the 1850's, ere the police system had been properly organised, and the old parish constables were still in existence, the mining towns were ill-equipped to cope with the gangs of riotous miners who not infrequently swept through the district when strikes and trade disputes disturbed the economic serenity of the district. At that time the Earl of Dudley was the largest mining magnate hereabouts, possessing nearly 400 pits and having 5,000 miners in his employ, and these chiefly on the Dudley and Rowley side of his property. The larger coalmasters of the vicinity also included Lord Dartmouth, Messrs. Dawes, Halford, and a score of others. During a notable strike in 1860 some twenty thousand miners took part, and eventually the military had to be called out to deal with the situation.

One mob, after spreading terror and consternation in Tipton, marched to Oldbury, where one of the first acts committed by the lawless band was to burst open the cells adjoining the old Court House, in which a few prisoners for debt were confined. These were all liberated, and they immediately put their liberty to use by taking a hasty departure from the scene of their incarceration.

PITS AND BATTLESHIPS *Tom Jones*

If you go up to SavaCentre and look at the old Ordnance Survey map you'll be surprised at how many mines were in this area. Most of Oldbury is built on pit spoil. There were more pits here than there were in the Valleys - there's no doubt about that. More than in the Rhondda and the Aberdare Valley put together - and the Merthyr Valley. But they weren't deep mine pits, they were house coal pits. Whereas the Welsh pits were steam coal, mainly, they were dug for coal for the battleships in the First World War. But these in Oldbury were open long before they even started in South Wales.

There is an Oldbury Connection with battleships, though. In the First World War the German Fleet was scuppered at Scapa Flow and it was Cox and Danks of Oldbury that raised those ships for salvage. They filled in the holes and then pumped them full of compressed air to float them. It was the first time that a battleship had ever been raised.

THE METROPOLITAN CARRIAGE WORKS *Wilfred Carter*

They used to build tanks for the 1914-18 war at the Metropolitan Carriage Works down the Broadwell. There was a piece of land at the back that we used to call the Tank Field. On the other side of the canal from the Carriage Works was a concrete slope where they used to test the tanks going up.

There was for many years a 1914-18 tank standing in the area that the War Memorial is in now. It disappeared at the time that they started work on the War Memorial.

THE SECRET WATER TANKS

In the interests of security the rumour was circulated that the Carriage Works was engaged in producing water tanks for the war effort, hence the name 'tanks'. The testing ground was Mill Farm, a small dairy farm which was requisitioned by the Army. After the war it reverted to farmland and continued as a working farm until the 1930's.

THE GENERAL STORE   *Mrs Conley*

General Store at the corner of Cyprus St and the bottom end of Bridge St.

The lady in the door is Agnes Tolley my grandmother. She died during the first world war. The photograph was taken just before the war.
Agnes Tolley and my aunt (now 97) could remember the tanks going down the road past the shop at around midnight. They used to come out of the carriage works,and down the farm track to the road. The noise they made was terrific.
I can remember the shop when it was owned by another family, possibly the Halligans.

During the Second World War the town was very busy with all the traffic coming through the centre. I worked at Accles & Pollock, as a typist in a works department. They made gun barrels, and there were aircraft parts made in the town during this war. We were very lucky in that we had very few airraids, especially with the chemical works being here. We would hold our breath because of worry about the chemical works being hit. There was a mixed gun battery on the top of Bury Hill. My father in law did fire watching there.

THE TANK ON THE TIP   *Alan Baxter*

I can just remember the tank being towed away when I was a child. They towed it off to a place just down the Dudley Road, approximately where the Birmingham Board Company is now, and just left it there on what looked like a rubbish dump. It's that that I remember best, the tank just sat there on this tip. My uncle was a saddler who lived in Freeth Street and he rode on it on that final journey. He would always talk of the tanks being taken out from the factory in the middle of the night to maintain security.

His business suffered from the closing of the coal mines in Rowley as he used to do the saddlery for them and lost the business of 3000 horses when they closed. The other disappointment for him and his wife was that they were led to believe that the opening of the New Road from Birmingham to Wolverhampton would take the traffic off all the other roads, and of course it did no such thing.

I suffered my own disappointment at the opening of the New Road. We were all there from school to see the Prince of Wales perform the opening. I was only 7 or 8 years old and I don't know what I expected to see, a man on a white horse come riding down the road? The sight of him arriving in 'just' a car was a real let down.

Where the Motorway crosses the Dudley Road now there used to be lime kilns. I can remember going to church on a Sunday and the smoke belching out from them. Looking down to the canal there was a boatyard. I don't actually remember the motorway being built though. I was working in Birmingham at the time and I can remember it being discussed, yet although I was travelling a lot I can't remember it coming. The first recollection I have of it is a car journey back from Worcester one foggy night and being so relieved that you could guarantee that there was nothing coming the other way.

During the Second World War I was going around with my aunt who was a warden to check that people knew how to put on their newly issued gas masks. One old man that we visited said, "I've got one but I shor wear one. I shall do the same as I did in the last one - suck a stone."

I was taking part in a Home Guard exercise, in 1943 or 44, on the football ground which is now Sandwell Borough's pitch at Oldbury Leisure Centre. We saw a little training plane, a little fabric training plane, going round above us. It circled and then came in to land on the pitch. A pilot who identified himself as Polish got out and asked us the way to Wolverhampton air field. When we told him he simply got back in and took off again.   31

One day we Home Guards were called out to the school over the road from St Hubert's church on Wolverhampton New Road as someone had thrown hand grenades into it. The Home Guard kept their ammunition in two sheds on the golf course and a gang of kids had broken into one of the sheds and stolen some of the grenades. It turned out that they had lobbed one into the school and nothing had happened because we never kept them primed. One of the kids had a father in the army and he said "Dad said that before you use them you have to put something else inside."

So they broke into the other shed and found the 'other bit', and somehow managed to put a live grenade together. They threw one into a bunker on the golf course and it went off sending sand up into the air .... all over the place!

Some of the very first phosphorous bombs that were dropped on Birmingham landed in the vicinity of Albright and Wilson. It was rumoured that the workers put them out by urinating on them, a rumour that was allowed to circulate because this was the sort of story they wanted to encourage to make it seem that the phosphorous bombs weren't very dangerous.

The tank being towed away by a traction engine belonging to Screen Brothers Ltd., of Brades Village.

EUSTACE THE NAUGHTY BARRAGE BALLOON

Enid Harvey

Now during the 1939 - 1946 war Barrage Balloons were flown around towns to make enemy planes fly higher, so that they couldn't pinpoint targets easily (there was no sophisticated equipment then like there is now). A Barrage Balloon looks something like an elephant without legs, trunk or tail, and was attached by wires to a winch on a lorry.

We (that was the children at the then Oldbury Technical School, just across the road from Broadwell Park) called this balloon Eustace and he used to be quite naughty at times. He used to make us lose our concentration during lessons because he used to fly away from his winch. We would look through the classroom window towards the park and watch the R.A.F. men looking after him trying to make him fat enough to fly. Sometimes something wouldn't go right and Eustace would keep himself thin, just like an ordinary balloon with a hole - perhaps he was tired! At other times he would grow fat and take off to fly quite nicely, for a while looking proud of himself - sometimes the sun would shine on Eustace and then he would shine silvery. When the wind was blowing Eustace would be tossed around - back and forth - this way and that - and he would buck and leap and tear himself away from his mooring. Up and away - just as if he was enjoying his freedom, with his wires trailing behind, catching on anything in his way.
The R.A.F. men would have to chase after him and when they had caught him bring him back to the park and start all over again. When they got Eustace back he looked sorry for himself, all flat and grey and the men would put the wires back in place and blow him up again. Time after time Eustace flew off - time after time he was brought back - but I think the R.A.F. must have got tired of his naughty antics because, before the war ended they had taken him away, but I had left school by this time so I didn't miss the lack of Eustace's distractions.

....

ABOUT MRS HARVEY

Davide Piras

Mrs Harvey started school at three and a half years old. Her parents lived in Smethwick for about 4 years, then her parents decided to move to Oldbury. At Oldbury Tech she played hopscotch, skipping and kick the can. She started school at 9.00 a.m. and finished at 4.00 p.m.

We started school at the age of four years old. I have lived in Oldbury all my life. I play football.

She goes to bed at 8.30 because she wants to get up, and she wakes up at 6.00 and for three hours she reads a book.

I go to bed at 10.00 and I wake up at 8.00 and I read for 30 minutes.

Davide Piras was a pupil of Christ Church Primary School.

SCHOOL IN THE 1930's   *Lucy Harbach & Nina Littler*

NAME: Mrs Constance Collins
AGE: 67 Years old.

She was born in Popes Lane on the 5th of August 1925. She was 5 years old when she went to school and she started work at 14. When she was at school all the children had a little white card. They had a sentence on the card. The children had to stand on their chair. She had to read the sentence standing on her chair. They had a different sentence on each card. She wrote on a slate with chalk. If it rained at play time they had a sand tray to play in. The teachers were very strict. If you were naughty you had 100 lines and you had to do them after school. She never had the cane but she had the pencil across her knuckles.

She walked to school every day. She started school at 9.00. She finished school at 4.30. She was the oldest and had to dress her brothers and sisters for bed. She went to bed at 9 o'clock. At school she played hopscotch, rounders and Jack Hatney. This is her best playground rhyme:

> " I like coffee
> I like tea
> I like sitting on a dustman's knee".

She had to eat porridge for breakfast, lunch, dinner, and tea. If you were naughty and didn't eat your dinner you were sent to bed and you had your dinner for your next dinner and it was put there until you ate it. She had lots of jobs like pulling the coal and scrubbing the floors every morning, and lived in a newspaper shop. When she had pocket money she only had half a penny. She spent her half a penny on sweets. You had 2 ounce for a penny so she got one ounce for half a penny. They had cone shaped bags. If you had two penny worth you had a square bag. If you had a square bag of sweets you were posh.

She said that she liked Oldbury best and she said that there is lots more greenery in Oldbury now than before.

Lucy Harbach and Nina Littler were pupils of Christ Church Primary School.
This is an editing together of their individual pieces of writing.

PORRIDGE FOR BREAKFAST   *Tina Cannon*

A comparison of diet in the 1930's and 1990's in verse.

I like chips
I like peas
I like sausage
I like beans

Porridge
Porridge
Porridge
Porridge
Porridge for breakfast
Porridge for tea

I like bread
I like eggs
I like pies
I like chicken legs

Porridge
Porridge
Porridge
Porridge
Porridge for breakfast
Porridge for tea

I like garlic
I like cheese
I like apple pie and custard
I like mushy peas

Porridge
Porridge
Porridge
Porridge
Porridge for breakfast
Porridge for tea

I like cabbage
I like swede
I like carrots
I like wheat

I like potatoes
I like meat
but they had

Porridge
Porridge
Porridge
Porridge
Porridge for breakfast
Porridge for tea

**Tina Cannon was a pupil
of Christ Church
Primary School.**

(To fully appreciate the reason that the above poem was written see the first line of the last-but-one paragraph on the previous page).

The small child at the front of the picture is Mrs Price's mother; behind is her Aunt Dolly; at the rear an unnamed employee; to his right Beatrice Roden (Mrs Price's Grandmother); John Roden (her Grandfather); and on the right Jack Roden who later ran the shop.

LIFE IN A PRINT SHOP   *Margaret Price*

My grandfather's print shop was at 38 Church Street, next to the Swan pub, and opposite the Wesley chapel. I lived at there with my grandparents and parents until my mother died in 1952. After that my father and I moved.

My grandfather founded the business and ran it until he died when my Uncle Jack took it over. Mother started up and ran the stationers shop at the front of the building and did all the proof reading to make sure there were no mistakes in the printed material. The printing was done in an outhouse in the yard - it came out into Back Lane. Downstairs was a printing press where they did posters etc., all the big printing jobs, while upstairs were trays of type and another machine. Our living quarters were at the back of the shop and I can remember the hymn sheets for the anniversaries being stapled together on the living room table. It was a big table and all of the collating and stapling was done there. The guillotine was in my bedroom, under the window. I remember Uncle Jack coming up to use it - not while I was in bed though!

CASH REGISTERS
Jennie Leek

The first cash register was a number of overhead wires leading from the assistants to the cashier's position. Metal containers in which money could be placed were catapulted along the wires. It was quite amusing to see and hear the little metal cups whizzing along their wire tracks. This system was used in George Mason's shop on the corner of Church Street and Birmingham Street.

Jennie Leek was a pupil of Tividale Comprehensive School.
(The above piece was written after conversations with Shirley Southall and Jean Counley).

THE PAWNBROKERS
Sukhbir Bal

Violet Evans worked for a pawnbroker and a jeweller. She got paid 80 pence a week for 40 hours. She did a lot of scrubbing at the pawnbrokers. She started work when she was 14. Violet walked it to work and back. It took her three hours. She went to bed at 6.00 and woke up at 5.45. She had to wake early to go to work. She did the sweeping at home and she babysat her brothers and sisters for 6 hours because they never went to sleep. Violet's best treat was to go to the pictures. There were moving pictures and a man playing the piano. There was no talking. If you talked you would get chucked out.

Sukhbir Bal was a pupil of Christ Church Primary School.

THE MARKET
Henry McKean

The right to collect tolls was acquired from the Lord of the manor. The first tolls were collected on February 9th 1895. The Local Board applied for and were granted a faculty to set back the fence of the garden, formerly a churchyard, to make room for the stalls without obstructing traffic. There is a very busy scene on Tuesday mornings and Saturday evenings. The tolls are satisfactory, and every year produce more than the original sum paid for the right to collect them.

from "Picturesque Oldbury" (1900).

RUNG AROUND WITH WATER

At one time it was impossible to enter Oldbury without passing over a canal.

Bustle Bridge, which stands today in 1994 an unnoticed hump in the road, was a structure which had a main road, in the form of Birmingham Street, running over it and buildings on either side of that road. Although the canal is now filled in it is still possible to see where it ran between the back of the health centre and the church of St Francis Xavier.

In 1767 an Act of Parliament authorised the cutting of a canal to link Birmingham and its' busy hardware industry with the collieries at Wednesbury. Till then the traffic of long trains of wagons laden with coals had ploughed up the roads and made the highways a dismal spectacle. The route chosen was through Birmingham Heath and Winson Green, through Smethwick and Oldbury, over Puppy Green and through Tipton and Bilston to join the Severn navigations beyond. The work was completed in 1769.

The easier and cheaper method of water-carriage, in boats holding 25 tons of coal, could not but give an impetus to the trade of the entire district, in which Oldbury reaped a full share of the advantages. And not only did the new artificial water-ways foster the traffic in raw minerals, but early in the nineteenth century Oldbury boasted blast-furnaces for the production of pig-iron, and steelworks, the heavy productions of which needed cheap freightage to ensure their prosperity. It was in 1824 that Thomas Telford made the last improvement to the local canal system before the canals were eclipsed by the railways.

In connection with the erection of certain iron bridges over the canal in the Birmingham district, the great Duke of Wellington paid his only visit to this part of the country in 1830. On this occasion his carriage was stoned by a mob owing to his opposition to the Bill for Catholic Emancipation. In company with Sir Robert Peel, he made a trip along the canal in the directors' state barge. At that time the canal company ran swift packet boats, drawn by three horses, for passenger traffic.

It was by this method of transport that the British Association, in 1839, made an excursion from Birmingham, where they were holding their annual conclave, to what Professor Phillips termed "those marvellous works of art, the Dudley Caverns," which, "by the liberality of Lord Ward," were illuminated on a grand scale by 1,600 dozen candles (see pg. 24).

At that time a covered "market boat", as it was called, drawn by two horses, plied three times a week between Birmingham and Wolverhampton. The time-bills which advertised the daily service of these "Swift Packets" between Birmingham and Wolverhampton were as fraudulently seductive as any advertisements of the kind could be. They were ornamented by a rough woodcut, which depicted a sort of gondola ploughing its watery way between finely wooded banks, and traversing a country of extraordinary natural beauty. As a matter of fact, the barge was a sort of elongated house-boat, drawn at a jog-trot by a pair of sorry steeds rope-harnessed to it, one of them ridden bare-backed by a Black Country urchin. While as to the landscape through which the journey was made, the best that can be said of it was - well, it was the newest and therefore the lightest fringe of the dingy Black Country. The inside of the boat was accounted "first class" accommodation, and the outside top of the cabin was "second class." It was a common practice for poor folk, journeying from town to town along the tow-path, to throw their loads or bundles to some friendly passenger on the outside deck, and to recover their property at the nearest lock to their destination - a cheap way of getting their luggage or marketings carried home, of which many an Oldbury man was wont to avail himself in those easy-going, simple minded days.

A Birmingham advertisement, of which the following is a copy, explains itself:-

EXCURSION TO DUDLEY CASTLE.
Admission Ticket, 1/6.
ON TUESDAY, JUNE 20TH, 1843,
the Packet starts from the
WAGON AND HORSES, FRIDAY BRIDGE,
at half-past six o'clock precisely.

These "fly-boats," as they were called, continued to ply regularly along the canal through Smethwick and Oldbury, until such time as they were superseded by the train service of the Stour Valley Railway, which line runs alongside this waterway for several miles of the distance.

It is a long cry from the days of ill-kept roads and slow, horse-drawn wagons to those of fast railways and express goods trains; it is the difference between an output of Jews' harps and clout nails and one of anvils and ships' anchors.

The above is based upon a passage from F. W. Hackwood.

OLD WHITE SWAN

MUSEUM,

CHURCH STREET

(*Nearly opposite the County Court*),

OLDBURY, near Birmingham.

BENJAMIN SADLER,

In tendering his grateful acknowledgments to his numerous friends for the liberal support bestowed upon him since taking to the above celebrated Museum, which stands unrivalled for its rare and beautiful collection of

NATURE'S WONDERS,

Begs to acquaint them that since his removal to his handsome and extensive premises, he has made many choice and valuable additions to his splendid collection of novelties, and hopes, by continually introducing scarce and rare specimens of Nature and Art to his already valuable Museum, to secure a continuance of their kind patronage and support.

The premises are splendidly fitted up, having recently been beautifully re-decorated, and the magnificent room contains, in addition to his collection of

Birds, Animals, Reptiles, and Insects,

A

POWERFUL MECHANICAL ORGAN,

thus rendering it the most attractive Museum in the Midland Counties.

WINES, SPIRITS, & REFRESHMENTS,

of the first quality, and at reasonable charges.

Admission Free. Open Daily.

Entry from "Littlebury's Worcestershire Directory" 1873.

Although the Swan pub was renowned for its collection of curios (see pg. 48) and later became the first cinema in Oldbury (an application being made for permission to undertake alterations to the building, in order to show films, in 1910), it was by no means the only such collection in the area as will be seen from the following extract: "There was at that time a capital collection of stuffed animals, open freely to the public, at the Windsor Castle Tavern, Rounds Green. In the absence of any municipally provided museum, who shall deny it a place of merit? Primitive times, primitive methods, and simple tastes soon satisfied".

THE SCHOOL OF HARD KNOCKS   *Sid Hill*

I'm 59 and, until the age of 14, was raised on a local barge. We were coming along the navigation one day and I said "I'd love to learn to swim dad". He said, "Would you?" I said "Yes please dad". "Right", he said, "Now's the time to learn. And he gave me a good slap along me legs and in I went. He said, "Now get out of that"s - and I did. It was either that or sink. I still can't swim but I can get out of the water alright.

A DAY AT THE RACES   *Joanne Price*

"A race course was very much part of the town," said Fred.
"In my day people came from outside Oldbury for a flutter and
a bit of conversation - not to mention the odd win now and again!
But whether a winner or not the place blazed with excitement, the
heat and the dust meant nothing. Each one of us named it our day.
We were equals with any other chap, rich or not. It was our Ascot
and we hoped it would last forever, no one would take it away."

This story was told to Joanne Price in a bar. The race course appears on no maps but as betting shops only became legal in 1961 this is hardly surprising!

SLOW DOWN FOR MISFITS   *Ray Billington*
(A town turned tortoise)

Soft flesh beneath a tough shell.
Older, perhaps, than the oldest man.
Slow mover, it needs time - lots of it.

Winter sleeper emerging with the green shoots.
No more than inches long, not a heavyweight,
nor has ever been.

A descendant, perhaps, of the giant reptiles.
Now, even, rather insignificant.
But nobody hates a tortoise, do they?

Ray Billington was District Librarian in charge of Oldbury from 1974-77.
(This poem was written during a workshop envisaging Oldbury as a living creature).   41

ODE TO ROWLEY HILLS*   *James Whitehouse*

Full oft on Cambria's breezy hills
      I've stood, and gazed upon the scene
Of rushing streams and sparkling rills,
      Of shady woods and meadows green.

And oft, upon some jutting peak,
      I've watched the vessels scudding by,
And heard the seagull's plaintive shriek,
      Like to a newborn infant's cry.

But still I love dear Rowley Hills,
      To rest upon their verdant brow,
When spring dispels old winter's chills,
      And starts to work the spade and plough.

I cannot stand upon their heights
      And view the ever-rolling sea,
But everywhere my eye alights
      Recalls some memory sweet to me.

And when the lark his song shall raise,
      At early dawn in grateful trills,
I'll join with his my humble praise,
      To Him who gave us Rowley Hills.

* Bury hill, situated in Oldbury, is a distinct spur from the Rowley range.

BLUE BILLY AND BASALT WINDOWSILLS   *Arthur Reeves*

Chance's used to make their own soda at their Smethwick Glassworks rather than buy it. When other people started to buy it from them they began to manufacture it at the Alkali Works, Oldbury. There used to be a gantry spanning the road and the waste would be transported across it from the factory to the tip. Blue Billy, as the tip became known, gave off gases so obnoxious that they affected people's health. My grandmother lived in Oldbury and she died young - I have a feeling that it was from acute asthma. Chance's wanted to move the factory because of the hazard but the people of Oldbury didn't want to see it moved because of the loss of jobs. Luckily a new process was started in the plant which eliminated the noxious waste. However Blue Billy remained. It was taken away after World War 2 and used for fertiliser and road making.

Glassmaking was brought to Oldbury when Chance Brothers decided to rationalise their site, concentrating on making sheet glass. William Edward Chance was given the option of taking over certain processes as long as he moved to another site. He chose Churchbridge, Oldbury. The company became best known for its stained glass and for glass bells, used to put over wreaths or flower arrangements on graves, or ornaments in the house. The windowsills at the Junction pub are reminders of another process from Chance Brothers. They are made from basalt. Rowley Rag was melted down and cast. It was meant for mantleshelves, but was never a commercial success as they couldn't compete with wood.

CHANCE, BROTHERS, & CO.   *J. Littlebury*

Manufacturers of soda-crystals, soda-ash, bi-carbonate of soda, sal-ammoniac, muriate and sulphate of ammonia, green copperas, sulphuric and muriatic acids, etc., etc., Alkali works.

The chemical works of Messrs. Chance, Brothers, and Co., and Messrs. Lewis Demuth and Co., the phosphorus works of Albright and Wilson, and the copper works of the Tharsis Sulphur and Copper Company, Limited, are all on a large scale. The Oldbury Wagon Works afford employment to a great number of hands. The Brades is an immense place, covering between eight and nine acres of ground, being so closely pitched and packed that the sight is almost bewildering to any one not familiar, from daily custom, with such scenes. Brick making also forms an important branch of manufacture in this locality. Patrick Allan Fraser, Esq., is lord of the manor and impropriator of the living. A court leet is held annually. Fairs are held on June 6th and October 3rd.

from "Littlebury's Worcestershire Directory 1873".

LIVING IN LOW TOWN

Mrs Violet Key

When I was a child we lived in the same street as Jack Judge's family in Low Town. He used to put on concerts at the old Town Hall in Oldbury. He had a little stall from which he would sell fish. It was opposite the church where 'Polly on the Fountain' used to be.

My father was the local undertaker, a business which my brother still continues in the town. Father, who learned his trade from Councillor John Wirtlee, also did some of the woodwork on houses in Moat Road.

I lived for 50 years in Church Square, working for a group of doctors at number 10, in the Square. This was originally the Dr's Mence. The Mence's had their own tennis court at the back in Canal Street. When the National Health Service came into being the Mence's refused to join and the business was bought by doctors Barrada, Hawson and Lockley.

Low Town, where I was brought up, was one of four streets at the bottom of Birmingham Street that were completely demolished to make way for the Oldbury Ring Road. The other three were Perrott Street, New Street and Green Street. The rest of the area is a car park now. The Fire Station used to be a little place on the corner of Low Town and Perrott Street, and there was a water man, a turncock, who lived on the corner of Perrott Street - I used to play with his daughter. My mother's uncle had a slate yard in Low Town. They were called Smith and Son and got their roofing slates from Bangor in North Wales.

The River Tame used to come above ground at the bottom of Low Town. It was only a little stream which soon went underground again and came out at Broadwell. As you came up from Low Town towards the centre of Oldbury you would go over Bustle Bridge, a bridge over the canal, which had buildings built on both sides of it. To get down to the canal you would go down a staircase which is at the side of where St David's Court is now. The canal was long since filled in and built over.

TAME WATERS

"Tame taketh its first beginning about Oldbury, being a mile or something more eastward from Dudley Castle."

Sampson Erdeswick. "Survey of Staffordshire" 1597.

MUSICAL OLDBURY .....

Jack Judge, (died 1938) who co-wrote the popular First World War song 'It's a Long Way To Tipperary' with Harry Williams, had a fish stall in Oldbury, on the piece of land outside the Junction pub, where 'Polly on the Fountain' stood. Although he penned many songs he never gave up the stall and sometimes put together a few lines while he was standing there to help him sell his fish.

John Frederick Bridge, who was organist at Westminster Abbey from 1882-1918, was born in Oldbury on December 5th 1844. He was baptised by the first vicar of Oldbury, The Reverend George Sproston, but left the town at the age of six when his father took up a position of Vicar-Choral at Rochester Cathedral. He composed music for the funeral of Darwin and set one of Tennyson's last poems 'Crossing the bar' to music for the poet's funeral in 1892. In 1923 he visited Rowley, where he had relatives, to open the new organ in the Parish Church. He died in 1924 and is buried near his home in Glass, Aberdeenshire.

Other Oldbury musicians include Joseph Hill, who became organist at Oxford University; Enoch Holloway, a great bass singer who won the Crystal Palace contest; and Theodore Pearsall, whose story follows.

..... INSTRUMENTAL OLDBURY

In 1935 the Department of Commerce of the United States reported that all the Jews Harps of the world were being made by one firm in Birmingham, England, that one order just given from the United States to this firm was for 160,000 instruments, and that the firm in question, though making 100,000 a week was unable to keep up with the world demand owing to a lack of skilled 'tongue-setters'.
The Oxford Companion to Music.

Another small item of production from the days when Birmingham was the toyshop of Europe is peculiar to this locality. At one time all the Jews' harps in the world were made in Rowley parish. The Barnsley's, of Cradley Road, were well-known makers. This instrument, for which the proper etymon is Jaws' harp, because it is played between the two jaws, is highly popular with the inhabitants of the lonely isle of St. Kilda. It is a primitive sort of musical instrument, the metal spring or vibrator producing only one note, all the variations to make the tune being effected by the player's mouth, the pitch of the note being capable of producing good musical intonations.
F. W. Hackwood

OLDBURY GENIUS WHOM THE WORLD MOURNED

THEODORE PEARSALL
DIED MARCH 9TH 1880, AGED 16 YEARS
AT BERLIN
WHERE HE WAS STUDYING AT THE
CONSERVATOIRE OF MUSIC. HIS SUCCESS
AS A VIOLINIST EXCITED THE ADMIRATION
OF THE MOST EMINENT MUSICIANS, AND
GAVE PROMISE OF A BRILLIANT FUTURE,
WHILST HIS PURE AND GENTLE DISPOSITION
ENDEARED HIM TO ALL WHO KNEW HIM.
THIS MONUMENT IS ERECTED
IN COMMEMORATION OF HIS WONDERFUL
GENIUS AND EXECUTIVE TALENT AND TO
REMIND THE YOUTHFUL GENERATION OF
THE SUCCESS WHICH ATTENDS A
LAUDABLE AMBITION AND A PERSEVERING
DEVOTION TO NOBLE AIMS.

HIS REMAINS ARE INTERRED IN THE CEMETERY
OF THE TWELVE APOSTLES, BERLIN.

It has been over 100 years since a handsome 16 year old, kissed his father goodbye and set off, with his violin, for the Imperial Conservatory of Music, Berlin, and the promise of world-wide fame as a master musician.

Theodore Pearsall was born in Popes Lane in a little detached cottage opposite the entrance to Jerram's brewery. Theodore's ancestors for generations on his mother's side were musicians. His great-grandfather, Mr W. Vernon, of Pelton Hall, Warwickshire, was a violinist, and his grandmother was accomplished on the piano and organ. His mother was a brilliant harpist, but never lived to see her son's fame - she died when he was about three. David Pearsall his father, was a violinist, and encouraged Theodore to develop his talent. When his son died, his heart was broken, and neighbours found it difficult to prevent him from committing suicide. Theodore's only brother, Ernest, was a pianist. He let his art decline, however, and died in his forties, having kept a fried fish shop in Moore Street, West Bromwich.

At the age of two, Theodore was familiar with the violin, but his musical education did not really commence until he was five. It was hard work to get him to go to the National Schools then, and he often played truant so that he could practise - which he did for six to eight hours a day. He was a good-looking lad, with light-brown hair and regular features, and the local schoolchildren would often take the rise out of him because of his dreamy, head-in-the-clouds behaviour. Because of his delicate hands, his father would not allow him to play the traditional games which were played in Tat Bank - marbles, tip-cat and "duck-on-the-hob" - but this did not worry him very much, and he found more than enough enjoyment in his music, and often played until two o'clock in the morning.

Before he was seven, Theodore made his first appearance in public, performing two of Henry Farmer's difficult solos "with astonishing accuracy". By the time he was nine he had mastered Krentzer, Rode, Fiorillo, Mayseder, and De Beriot, studying under his father who then worked for Chance's in Halesowen Street. Henry Hayward, of Wolverhampton, next became his tutor, and at the classical chamber concerts held in that town he was an especial favourite.

To preserve his hands, Theodore was never caned for his frequent absences from the National Schools, but he made some recompense by giving his assistance at concerts there on more than one occasion. Needless to say, even his frustrated teachers had to admit that they appreciated his playing!

In April 1878, he entered as a student in the London Academy of Music, and his progress was so rapid that he was chosen to illustrate lectures on great composers, his performances winning the admiration of both students and professors. He also played - privately - before some of the greatest musical authorities in the country. He played to the appreciative ears of Dr. Stainer, of St. Paul's, Madame Norman Neruda, Princess Mary of Teck, the Duke of Marlborough, and Earls Beaconsfield, Bradford, Aberdeen and Lord Claude Hamilton. In open competitions Theodore walked off with all the honours of the Academy.

The time was ripe for him to finish off his tuition on the continent and Mr. Charles Halle - his admirer and adviser - made arrangements for him to go to Berlin to study under Professor Joachim. What an event in Theodore's young life! He was then only 16, and growing fast - he was about 5ft. 8ins., and very slim. He had adoring friends and supporters all over the country, and he was 'mad about his music'.

Then at the Imperial Conservatory, on March 9th 1880, the blow fell. The dreamy boy genius, born amid the smoke and grime of Oldbury, and destined, perhaps to rank with Paganini, Kreisler and Menuhin as a master of the world's loveliest art, died suddenly, from 'palpitation of the heart', while his greatness was still in the bud. Although always of a delicate constitution, his father had recently been assured by some eminent surgeons that he was not affected by any disease, and he had, only a few days before, written to his father saying how much his health had improved.

News of his untimely death resounded through the elegant salons, stately concert halls and elegant opera houses of Europe. But it was never more heartfelt as in the rough-and-tumble concert halls of Oldbury, his native town. Theodore Pearsall was mourned in the places in which he was "too class" to play - in the "White Swan" in Church Street, known as "The Bird Show", to which people came from miles around to see the butterflies, the stuffed birds, the young lion and the pig with six legs. Theodore's brilliant playing never blended with the big organ at the back of the "Bird Show" which warranted a quart of ale to the man who could wind it up with one hand. But the humble musicians who played there mourned him, as they did at "Showell's Top Shop" at the top of the town, and the "Bustle House" on the bridge. And some of them were among the musicians who crammed the Town Hall with willing subscribers for the monument on which the above words are inscribed, the tall monument which today commands the entrance to Oldbury parish Church. At that meeting his former teacher Henry Hayward said that he had "never met one so young who played on the violin in such a masterly manner. And a Mr Rickards, from Birmingham Grammar School went on to say that Theodore was the first English boy to succeed in obtaining a scholarship in open competition at the Berlin Academy of Music.

At his graveside in Berlin's Church of the Twelve Apostles, three hundred and seventy of his fellow violinists mourned the loss of a prodigy with that rare qualification - "of pure and gentle disposition".

Based on an article in the Smethwick Telephone, Sat. 15th Jan. 1949, and earlier material..

SOURCES

Many of the publications from which extracts in 'Oldbury: The Town of the Four Moons' are taken can be found at the Sandwell Community History and Archives Service based at Smethwick Community Library.

Most reminiscence and original writing about Oldbury is from 'The Changing Face of Oldbury' a community book kept at Oldbury Community Library; and 'Beneath 4 Moons' a series of illuminated panels of text from Sandwell.

Other writing is specifically for this publication, or from private collections.